MY CUP RUNNE

(Most of the

Delia Halverson

My Cup Runneth Over (Most of the Time)

Devotions for Teachers

DIMENSIONS
FOR LIVING
NASHVILLE

MY CUP RUNNETH OVER (MOST OF THE TIME)
Devotions for Teachers

This book is printed on recycled, acid-free, elemental-chlorine-free paper.

Library of Congress Cataloging-in-Publication Data

Halverson, Delia Touchton.
My cup runneth over (most of the time) : Devotions for teachers / Delia Halverson.
p. cm.
ISBN 0-687-05692-6
1. Christian teachers—Paryer-books and devotions—English
I. Title.
BV4596.T43H35 1999
242'.68—dc21 98-36979
CIP

99 00 01 02 03 04 05 06 07 08 — 10 9 8 7 6 5 4 3 2

MANUFACTURED IN THE UNITED STATES OF AMERICA

To

all the teachers

who helped form

my faith

Contents

My Cup Bubbles with Everyday Events

My Cup Is Filled by Others

Introduction

Professional and volunteer teachers are special people. However, each of us is actually a teacher, whether we realize it or not. We teach intentionally and unintentionally. We teach children, youth, and adults. We teach specifics, and we also teach attitudes.

So you are a teacher! You know the joys and pleasures of seeing new thoughts and ideas bloom. You, like a gardener, prepare the soil, plant the seed, and provide the nourishment for growth. Also like a gardener, you are not responsible for the growth. God gives the growth.

My hope is that this little book can serve a threefold purpose:

- Show appreciation to you, as a teacher.
- Give you encouragement in your teaching experience.
- Help you recognize the many opportunities that abound for you to share God as you teach.

Delia Halverson

God Fills My Empty Cup

1
Lift me up when I'm weary, Lord.

But those who trust the Lord will find new strength. They will be strong like eagles soaring upward on wings; they will walk and run without getting tired.
Isaiah 40:31 (Contemporary English Version)

Oh, to have the energy of children! They run and play until they drop. Sometimes it seems that there are more pressures and responsibilities than I can endure, with lesson plans, needs of students, records to keep, and then my own personal life.

As a young adult, my daughter once called on the phone. The first thing she said was, "I wish I were a kid again!" To be sure, children have problems, and sometimes we don't recognize the importance of those problems to them. But they also have an unsuppressed ability to move outside those problems and enjoy times of total release, a time of uncontrolled joy!

It reminds me of the child who asked to be left alone with his baby brother. Fearful of the sibling rivalry they'd read about, the parents listened from behind the door. The child asked the baby, "Will you remind me again of what God is like? It's been awhile since I've been there."

We so often push ourselves away from God's support. When we accept that support, we soar upward as on eagle wings and recapture a child's ability to experience uncontrolled joy.

Reflect

What are the unnecessary worries in your life?

Where in your schedule can you WRITE IN a block of time to totally release your problems and experience uncontrolled joy?

Pray

God of joy, bring times of release into my life. Create in me, again, the heart and excitement of a child, even during times of pressure. Amen.

2
Thank you, Lord, for helping me.

At that time the Holy Spirit will tell you what to say.
Luke 12:12 (Contemporary English Version)

One lovely fall day, as I was unpacking workshop materials at a church in Tennessee, I panicked. My note cards were nowhere to be found. For weeks I had carefully planned my presentation, making note cards to help me along. Searching for a second time, I found my handout sheets, my display items, and my posters, but no note cards. I must have left them at home on my desk, a hundred miles away.

Just before a workshop I try to take a few minutes to commit my presentation to God, asking for guidance. This time it was more than a simple commitment. It was a desperate prayer for help! The verse from Luke came to my mind. In desperation I prayed, "OK, God, this is the time when the Holy Spirit will have to take over, for sure, if these folks are going to get any benefit from our time here together."

As the teachers moved into the room, I felt a surprising calm come over me. Gone was the panic, and I knew that God and I would manage quite nicely. After all, God can work miracles!

Reflect

When have you found yourself in a situation where you could no longer rely on your own ability to complete a task?

What can you do to help you remember to allow God to take over the situation for you? (Take a deep breath, recite a verse, or something else that helps.)

Pray

God, thank you for your way of helping me through the Holy Spirit. When I push the panic button, help me remember that you are the connecting wire between me and the help I need. Amen.

3
Lord, guide me in my lesson plans.

Show me your paths and teach me to follow; guide me by your truth and instruct me.

Psalm 25:4-5a (Contemporary English Version)

I looked around the room in frustration. I could not find my study guide. How could I prepare the lesson without the guide? My desk looked as if a tornado had hit it. Or rather, it looked as if the tornado had hit somewhere else and dumped it all on my desk.

The one thing that seemed to be uncovered was my little sign, "Go to your desk as to an altar." I've kept this suggestion somewhere near my desk since I was in college. It has helped me remember that all that I do should be dedicated to God, as I would bring it to an altar.

This time, as I read the words, I looked around and thought, "Is this the way I should treat an altar before God?" I took a moment to pray for serenity, and then began clearing things on my desk. I unearthed mail I'd received several weeks before and wondered why I'd kept it. There was a book from the church library I'd not read. And, of all things, a pair of sunglasses pushed under my "to do" file. As I discovered the missing study guide, I stopped before the desk-altar to praise God. Amazing how easy my lesson planning went that night!

Reflect

- Where do you work on your lesson plans?

- How might you approach your work space as an altar?

Pray

Lord of wisdom and Lord of order, help me look at my preparation time as a worship experience with you. Draw me close to you in this time at the desk-altar, and give me insight and direction. Amen.

4
God, I need a quick fix for this problem!

You are my God and protector. Please answer my prayer. I was in terrible distress, but you set me free. Now have pity and listen as I pray.

Psalm 4:1 (Contemporary English Version)

Sometimes I become very provoked with the amount of time it takes for the process of decision making. This seems particularly true in a church or on a school board. As a child, when I became impatient, my father gave me advice, "Little folks want what they want right now, but big folks can afford to wait."

Impatience is a very human trait. We'd all like to have things taken care of immediately. We look for a "quick fix" for our problems. The disciples must have tried Jesus' patience, for often he said such things as, "Don't any of you know what I am talking about by now?" (Matthew 15:16) or, "If you have ears, pay attention! Listen carefully to what you hear!" (Mark 4:23-24*a*). Do you hear yourself in the classroom using such words? But in each case, Jesus went right back and explained it again, often with another parable.

As the first verse of Psalm 4 indicates, David became

impatient with God when his prayers weren't answered. However, by the end of Psalm 4, as in most of the psalms, David recognizes God's loving care, even when his prayers are not answered as he'd like them to be. Verse 8 says, "I can lie down and sleep soundly because you, LORD, will keep me safe."

Reflect

What is a problem or situation that you'd currently like a quick fix for?

What impact will a slower approach to the situation make, if any?

Will a quick fix make a difference ten years from now?

Pray

Be patient with me, God, even when I lose my patience. I recognize that you are on my side, no matter what. Amen.

5
Sometimes I don't feel very wise, Lord.

You will say the wrong thing if you talk too much—so be sensible and watch what you say.
Proverbs 10:19 (Contemporary English Version)

I did it again. Will I ever learn? I really don't feel very wise when I begin talking before I allow a student to explain. Then I feel as if I'm a fool to retract what I've said. But I must do it in order to right myself with the student, and also in order to right myself with God.

Some people think *before* they talk, and some (like me) think *while* they talk. As teachers, we sometimes feel uncomfortable with silences after we ask a question. We're afraid the student hasn't learned, and so we rush in with the answer or with a judgment. But we must remember that sometimes students must think before they can answer.

We often forget that *we* must think before we talk, or at least listen to what the other person has to say. I believe that our rushed lifestyles also complicate the problem. We constantly have our minds on the next event, instead of focusing all of our attention on what's happening right now. We could save ourselves a lot of grief if we'd take time to listen before speaking or passing judgment.

Reflect

When have you spoken too soon and regretted it later?

If you are to be an instrument of God, how can you learn what God wants you to say in such situations?

Pray

My God, help me stop and listen so that I may hear what is being said by my students, and also so that I may hear what is being said by you in every situation. Amen.

6
God, I'm just too tired to pray!

In certain ways we are weak, but the Spirit is here to help us. For example, when we don't know what to pray for, the Spirit prays for us in ways that cannot be put into words.
Romans 8:26 (Contemporary English Version)

It had been a grueling day of labor, both physical and mental. It seemed that everything that could go wrong did, both at home and on the class project. This was a day I was glad to see come to an end. As I sank into my bed that night, I thought of praying, but words simply would not come to my head.

I woke the next morning, aching in body and hazy in mind. I began my usual early morning swim in the community pool with the intentions of working the kinks out of my arms and legs, but all I could do was float on top of the water and look to the sky. As I lay there, a peace came over me, and I knew that God was there with me. Or you might say the Holy Spirit was there, the part of God that lives within us. Words of a prayer still did not come to my mind, but I recognized that I was praying, communicating with God. There were no special thoughts. It was simply a state of being, a state of deep relationship with God.

Some time later I came across the above verse in Romans. I'd read it before, I'm sure, even studied it with a group. But now I read it with understanding. What a wonderful gift we have, a God who comes to us even when we are too tired to form words. A God who knows every ache of our tired bodies and every struggle of our brains.

When we feel we're simply too tired even to pray, the Holy Spirit takes over for us, if we simply allow it to happen. Those are sometimes the most meaningful experiences with God.

Reflect

Recall a time when you felt you were unable to reach out to God.

Were you trying too hard? How could you have done better at reaching for God?

Pray

My God, come to me and simply dwell within me. I need no more than to know you are here. Amen.

7
Lord, I've had it up to here!

I wish I had wings like a dove, so I could fly far away and be at peace.

Psalm 55:6 (Contemporary English Version)

There comes a time when I've simply had enough. Then I know I must take a sabbath. In God's wisdom we are made so that we need periodic breaks. This has been brought out from the beginning of time. The creation story exemplifies this, as do many rules of Hebrew law in the Old Testament. However, I firmly believe that what is sabbath time for one person may not be sabbath time for another.

When our livelihood and everyday activities involve physical labor, then a sabbath of physical rest is certainly in order. But when we, as teachers, employ our minds instead of muscles each day, then we need some physical activity for our sabbath. In either case, we do need to set aside some time to praise God, privately and corporately.

The trouble comes when we look at the sabbath as a rule instead of a voluntary choice. We must choose to follow our sabbath or it is not effective. Then there is joy in the sabbath. Then it is refreshing, energizing us for the six days of work to follow.

Reflect

What sort of sabbath do I need to build into my schedule? When?

How can I include private and corporate praise of God in my sabbath?

Pray

My God, you made me so that I require the break of a sabbath. Nudge me to take that time, and prompt me in my use of your sabbath. Amen.

8
O God, I need more hours in my days.

But I trust you, LORD, and I claim you as my God. My life is in your hands.

Psalm 31:14-15*a *(Contemporary English Version)

The day had been a blur of events. After teaching, I rushed from one meeting to an appointment, from the appointment home to prepare a meal, and then to church for another meeting in the evening. When would I work on the final plans for my next class? When would I write a letter to my relatives? When would I find time to clean house?

When my schedule gets hectic I bask in remembering the one time in my adult life when I felt I was "caught up." I specifically recall sitting on the back porch with my children and thinking, "There is really nothing that I have to do today." I can visualize the community, the house, and even the ages of my children. But that's the only time I can recall such a phenomenon.

There are just too many things that I enjoy doing, and too many folks I want to be with. I find it a constant struggle to continually prioritize my activities. Jesus spoke of this when he suggested that his friend Martha take the time to enjoy a conversation with him and Mary. The problem was not the jobs that Martha saw as so important, but the fact that she let those jobs take priority when there was a better choice for her time right then.

God sees life as a whole. We see life as little segments and try to piece as many segments into the puzzle as we possibly can. Sometimes we try to jam the pieces together so rapidly that we pile them on top of each other or break the pieces and ruin the whole picture.

Reflect

Review your activities this week. Of each activity, ask, How does that fit into God's plan for my life?

Choose one activity that is not necessary to carry out God's plan in your life and concentrate on eliminating it. Then move on to another one. Remember, it takes six weeks to break a habit!

Pray

God, help me center my life on you. I trust you so that I want to put my life—even my time schedule—into your hands. Amen.

9
God, draw me closer to you.

Please listen, God, and answer my prayer! I feel hopeless, and I cry out to you from a faraway land. Lead me to the mighty rock high above me.

Psalm 61:1-2 (Contemporary English Version)

There are times when we can't believe that God can be very close because we feel so helpless. We feel that God is "high above us" in the mighty rock, or in heaven, whatever that may be! God is so awesome that we can't recognize that God can also be personal.

In early biblical accounts, we read of a very personal relationship between God and people. Abraham spoke to God often, and Jacob even wrestled with God and had his name changed to Israel. Moses had a very personal experience at the burning bush, and Samuel heard God as a child. The Hebrews drifted away from the personal relationship with God when they placed intricate details of religious practice as the goal in life instead of simply looking to God. Jesus recognized this and reintroduced us to the personal aspect of God by referring to God as Abba, or Daddy, the family word for father.

The personal relationship makes our understanding of God different from that of many other religions. We recognize that God is interested in each of us personally, and we can feel comfortable asking for God's attention, just as the psalmist did.

Reflect

How can you help your students recognize that God is personally interested in each of us?

If students look up to teachers, how can you exhibit God's personal love?

Pray

My God, draw me to you as a parent draws a child into loving arms. Help me feel your arms around me, helping me through the pain of growing spiritually. Amen.

10
I need you now, as well as later, Lord.

Surely goodness and mercy shall follow me all the days of my life, and I shall dwell in the house of the Lord my whole life long.

Psalm 23:6 (New Revised Standard Version)

As I read this version of the Twenty-third Psalm, I recognized a new meaning. I grew up in the era of the King James and Revised Standard Versions of the Bible, where the verse reads *"I shall dwell in the house of the Lord forever."* I had always interpreted the end of this verse as a reference to "going to heaven and being with God." "The house of the Lord" meant either the church building or heaven. Logically, I saw "forever" as after death.

But this new version speaks of dwelling in the house of the Lord "my whole life long." In this version, I live with God all my life, from birth to death. God is beside me, to help me through the classroom hours, through the time of preparation, and through the trials of discipline. Only a teacher knows how many times we need to turn to God in our classrooms. Only a teacher knows the helplessness we encounter when we cannot find our lesson plan, or when we are confronted by a disgruntled parent. No matter what happens, God is there, encouraging us, urging us, crying with us. But God is also there, shouting for joy! Our classroom is also the house of the Lord, for all of our lives.

Reflect

When do you forget that God is with you and fail to ask for help?

What were the occasions of joy in the past few weeks? Did you share that joy with God?

Pray

My God, when I remember that you keep me in your house at all times, then I feel that my cup runneth over, even during the trials. You are truly the foundation of life. Help me to make you my foundation too. Amen.

11
Violence abounds, Lord. Do you care?

Look and be amazed at what's happening among the nations! Even if you were told, you would never believe what's taking place now.

Habakkuk 1:5 (Contemporary English Version)

Read this quote from a man who looked at what was going on around him. Does it sound familiar to you? Have you felt like praying this prayer?

> Our Lord, how long must I beg for your help before you listen? How long before you save us from all this violence? Why do you make me watch such terrible injustice? Why do you allow violence, lawlessness, crime, and cruelty to spread everywhere? Laws cannot be enforced; justice is always the loser; criminals crowd out honest people and twist the laws around.

In the United States each day violence is evident all around us. Every ten seconds child abuse or neglect is reported, and every seven hours one dies from this abuse or neglect. Every fourteen seconds a child or youth is arrested—every four minutes for a violent crime. Every two hours a child or youth is killed by firearms, and every four hours a child or youth commits suicide.

We see it as teachers, and we'd rather overlook it and not have to confront it. Often we try to fool ourselves by saying it doesn't happen in our neighborhood or school or church. But it does.

Reflect

The prayer printed above was not written during our lifetime. In fact, it comes from the Old Testament book of Habakkuk (1:2-4). Recognize that God loves us all and does not want such violence. Think about how unhappy God must have been in Habakkuk's time with the violence and how unhappy God must be today. Yet God gave humans individual wills, and God allows us to choose for ourselves how we will live.

Reread God's answer to Habakkuk above. There is good in the world. How can you affirm the good that is there, and how can you help just one person to practice peace and justice instead of violence? This will make God happy.

Pray

Lord, I would like to be your advocate for peace instead of violence. Show me the way. Amen.

God's Cup of Nourishment

12
Do I hear you calling me, God?

One day, Moses was taking care of the sheep and goats of his father-in-law Jethro, the priest of Midian, and Moses decided to lead them across the desert to Sinai, the holy mountain. There an angel of the LORD appeared to him from a burning bush. Moses saw that the bush was on fire, but it was not burning up. "This is strange!" he said to himself. "I'll go over and see why the bush isn't burning up."

When the Lord saw Moses coming near the bush, [God] called him by name, and Moses answered, "Here I am."

God replied, "Don't come any closer. Take off your sandals—the ground where you are standing is holy. I am the God who was worshiped by your ancestors Abraham, Isaac, and Jacob."

Moses was afraid to look at God, and so he hid his face.

Exodus 3:1-6 (Contemporary English Version)

God calls each of us uniquely. Jacob's call was so physical that he actually wrestled with God (Genesis 32:22-31). Samuel heard God call in the night, and he didn't recognize that call until his mentor, Eli, helped him interpret the call (1 Samuel 3:1-10). Paul's calling was also very physical, leaving him blind for a period of time (Acts 9:1-19). Timothy's calling came over a long period of time, as his mother and grandmother nurtured him in the faith (2 Timothy 1:3-5).

As teachers, we are called to teach more than facts and figures. We are also called to be caregivers and advocates of the faith. Sometimes God calls and calls, and we ignore the call or try to run away, as Jonah did (Jonah 1 and 2). It may take a crisis, such as Jonah's storm, to get our attention. But God continues to call when there is a mission for us to do.

Reflect

How has God called you?

Is there an additional calling that you try to ignore?

Pray

God, I thank you for calling me to teach. Although there are times when I wonder why you called me, I rejoice in the opportunity to serve you. Amen.

13
I'd like to know you better, Lord.

Can two people walk together without agreeing to meet?
Amos 3:3 (Contemporary English Version)

Interesting, the conversations you can overhear when students don't know you're close enough to hear. Two middle school girls sat near me and continued their conversation about a boy in the class. One of the girls really wanted to get to know the boy, but she was afraid to talk to him, although she had had several opportunities. The other girl said, "You'll never get to know him unless you talk to him!"

It reminded me of the way we often pray to God. We timidly recite a memorized prayer from our childhood, or we only take time to make some request for help. Then we say, "God never talks to me, and I just can't seem to pray."

As the girls realized, there is no way that we can get to know a person unless we carry on a conversation. And a true conversation is not one-sided. We must take time to listen, too. It is only through learning of God in the Scriptures and spending time, one on one, with God that we become better acquainted.

There is a story of a young boy who stood in the door of

his father's study. When his dad finally realized that he was there, he asked, "Can I do something for you?"

The boy smiled and said, "Nope. I'm just lookin' and lovin'."

Unless we spend time lookin' and lovin' we'll never become acquainted with God.

Reflect

How much time did you spend simply lookin' at and lovin' God last week?

What is some object that you see frequently or some regular activity that you can use as a reminder to spend time with God?

Pray

My God, the prophets learned to talk with you, and Amos hadn't even been trained as a prophet. I want to try to set aside time to know you better. Amen.

14
How do I pray, Lord?

When you pray, don't be like those show-offs who love to stand up and pray in the meeting places and on the street corners. They do this just to look good. . . . When you pray, go into a room alone and close the door. . . . When you pray, don't talk on and on as people do who don't know God. They think God likes to hear long prayers.

Matthew 6:5-7 (Contemporary English Version)

The disciples asked Jesus' advice on prayer, and he gave them several suggestions, including a model prayer that we now call the Lord's Prayer.

As teachers we recognize that students express themselves in different ways, but sometimes we get stuck in an old mode of thinking when it comes to prayer. We think that everyone should pray in the same manner. Perhaps you have a friend who speaks of the spiritual experience he or she encounters in prayer, but you fear "diving into" prayer, afraid that you will fail to have the same spiritual experience.

In reality, we can't expect to have the same spiritual experience as someone else, because God made each of us unique. We all reach out to God in different ways, and God comes to each of us in a way that is distinctive to each person. We may spend private time with God in the morning or evening, or perhaps on a lunch break. And we may pray best by blocking out an entire morning or even a whole day for conversation with God.

The same is true with our method of prayer. You may find someone else's model of prayer meaningful to you, or you may need to develop your own. And you may need alternate ways of praying at different times. Try soothing music, and times of silence. Search out various locations in your home and outdoors.

However and wherever you pray, you will find God there, waiting for you—God, our ever-present help.

Reflect

What place do you feel closest to God? Why?

If you had a friend you wanted to know better, how would you go about it?

Can you take the same course for getting to know God better?

Pray

I truly want to know you better, Lord. Time is so short, but important things can always be worked into a schedule. I will make every effort to find time. Amen.

15
Lord, did you make me this way?

Don't be like the people of this world, but let God change the way you think. Then you will know how to do everything that is good and pleasing to [God].

Romans 12:2 (Contemporary English Version)

"I'm sorry, but that's the way I am. Take me or leave me."

There was a time not too long ago when we felt that such a statement justified our actions. We claimed that everyone is molded in childhood and not to be altered, and we were to accept our personalities and live with them. Although we were encouraged to get to know ourselves, we were never urged to take the step further and change the parts of our personalities that were irritating or offensive to others.

Charlie W. Shedd, in his book *Letters to Karen,* offered this advice to his daughter, "Maturity is in part knowing where you need to become more mature."

An evaluation of anything must be acted upon. A teacher who has students with discipline problems every year may be evaluated and given suggestions on ways to improve. The evaluation is of no use, however, unless it is put to work. There must be change in the teaching methods, or problems will continue to surface.

Granted, there are certain things about a teacher or a teaching situation that cannot be changed. There are time and classroom restraints. Budgets may put a limit on equipment or curriculum. Family situations can make a difference. All these situations must be worked around. But in order to perform as a complete person, we must learn our unchangeable circumstances and work with them. And we must learn to change the things that are changeable.

Maturity rises *above* such statements as, "But that's the way I am," and makes changes where change is possible. Changes come hard, but they can come about when they are directed by God and lubricated with love.

Reflect

When have you reacted to a constructive suggestion with the words or thoughts, "Well, that's just the way I am; take it or leave it!"

Which of those situations could you change for the better? How?

Pray

God, you know the true me. You know when the false me needs to be changed. Help my inability to see the need for change. Be my changing agent. Amen.

16
Sometimes I feel I learn more than my students!

Teach me to follow you, and I will obey your truth. Always keep me faithful.

Psalm 86:11 (Contemporary English Version)

It was a theme I'd dealt with very little, and a scripture I'd avoided. It was required in my college courses, but I was still struggling with the concepts. The book of Revelation seemed just too complicated for me. I rationalized that with all the scriptures in the Bible, my study time would be more productive if I worked with more positive passages.

And then the challenge came, from a student. He had heard a preacher at another church and was convinced that the electronic bar codes that were being installed in the grocery store were the "mark of the beast" as mentioned in Revelation. He knew that these bar codes would soon be applied to our hands or foreheads, and he wanted to share his discovery in our Bible study that next night.

I spent the evening and much of the next day in study and prayer. I went into the class the next night with fear and trepidation. Was I ready for this? I felt God working through me as I shared my learnings from Revelation. The young man never mentioned the electronic bar codes at all.

The big discovery I made was that I learned more by teaching than I had ever learned as a student in all the Bible courses I had had in college. Whether it's because of our special need as teachers, or because we are also hungering for understanding, we teachers seem to learn far more than our students.

Reflect

In your preparation for teaching a class, what new insights have you gained?

Think of the combination of discovering new insights of God and the joy of sharing those insights with students.

Pray

God, I thank you for the opportunity for such a rich ministry. The rewards of drawing closer to you and seeing new insights unfold for my students give me joy beyond words. Continue to be my guide. Amen.

17
Why give us free will, God?

Each one of you is part of the body of Christ, and you were chosen to live together in peace. So let the peace that comes from Christ control your thoughts. And be grateful. Let the message about Christ completely fill your lives, while you use all your wisdom to teach and instruct each other.
Colossians 3:15-16a (Contemporary English Version)

Sometimes it seems that God really goofed by giving us a will of our own. I especially feel that way when I've had a stormy encounter with my students. Wouldn't it have been much easier for everyone if God had made us all so that we would always do what is "right"?

Then I remember that God didn't make us as puppets. We are made in the image of God, and freedom of choice is a part of that image.

Many have said that they can't understand how there is so much evil in the world if there is a God. What's really surprising is that there is so much good when there are so many humans, each with a free will.

Reflect

What would the world be like if we were all "programmed" to act in a certain way?

What is special or unique about each of the students you teach?

How can you express love for each student, even when you do not approve of some actions?

Pray

God, you gave us each an individual will. You do not hold your love from us, even when we misuse that freedom. Help me love each person for the true person, not for the way he or she acts. Help me remember that I can love the person without loving the action. Amen.

18
Lord, thank you for an inquiring mind.

But put God's work first, and these things will be yours as well.
Luke 12:31 (Contemporary English Version)

Some teachers teach math, some history, some English, and some the Bible. Recently I realized how close the understanding of languages is to the understanding of the Bible. I'd known for years that persons translating the Bible had to understand the original biblical languages and be able to transfer the meanings into our words, but it didn't register just how important it is for me to understand meanings of words in my own language in order to grasp the translated Word.

The action verb *seek* is an example. One of the few verses I was ever able to memorize was Luke 12:31. The version I memorized said, "Seek ye the kingdom of God; and all these things shall be added unto you" (King James Version).

I usually associate seeking with something that is lost or absent. However, using my computer-age thesaurus I came up with a better understanding of the word. I found nine words listed: *pursue, try, follow, quest, query, inquire, request, ask, solicit.* None of them implied that the thing being sought was lost. I was particularly interested in the words *follow* and *quest*. Upon looking up "quest," I found *research* and *inquiry*, and the word *research* led me to *study*.

What a revelation for a teacher! The kingdom of God is an ongoing search, an opportunity to come to God with an inquiring mind. I like this "kingdom of God"!

Reflect

What inquiry have you been hesitant about using in your spiritual growth?

Find a favorite verse and use a thesaurus to discover the various meanings of some of the words.

Pray

God, give me the courage to seek you and to continue to grow through an inquiring mind. Amen.

19
How can I be more creative, God?

Each of you is now a new person. You are becoming more and more like your Creator, and you will understand [God] better.
Colossians 3:10 (Contemporary English Version)

In the first chapter of Genesis we read how God, the ultimate creator, made humans in God's own image. That being the case, then each of us is certainly capable of creativity. In Romans 12:6, we are told that God has given each of us different gifts or talents to use. Yet at times we feel that we have no talents. We excuse ourselves, saying, "Oh, that's for the creative ones. They're the ones with all the talents." Yet, just what is creativity? Did God give creativity to a select few? Can't we all be creative?

To be creative we need not produce something that society has never seen before. In fact, any time that you create something, then it is original to you. It's something new to you, whether anyone else in the world is familiar with it or not. *You* created it!

Creativity produces excitement, growth of the person, and a great deal of pleasure. Creativity is inside *us,* not in the thing that we produce. So we can all be creative, and we should strive for creativity in order to keep alive the excitement, growth, and pleasure of life.

Reflect

Barbara Bruce, in her book *The Creative Church,*[*] suggests the following characteristics of creative people. Which do you have?

Willing to take risks
Humorous and fun loving
Open-minded
Turns things around to improve them
Curious
Childlike
Questions assumptions
Looks for continuous improvement
Flexible
Tolerant of ambiguity
Willing to see both sides of an issue
Intuitive
Defers judgment
Spontaneous
Can see possibilities in existing things

How can you practice these characteristics more?

Pray

Creator God, you set me in your own image, and a part of that image is an ability to be creative. Free me to practice that creativity in my teaching. Through your guidance, I'll try to make the learning experience new and fresh, with the excitement of knowing you. Amen.

* Barbara Bruce, *The Creative Church* (1994), p. 27 (InterActive Resources, Inc., 1512 Roundhill Court, Nashville, TN 37211).

20
Make me wise, my God.

Anyone who hears and obeys these teachings of mine is like a wise person who built a house on solid rock. Rain poured down, rivers flooded, and winds beat against that house. But it did not fall, because it was built on solid rock.
Matthew 7:24-25 (Contemporary English Version)

With today's ever-changing world, it is important that we recognize the difference between being knowledgeable and being wise. Scholastic tests and trivia games measure knowledge. And in today's world, knowledge is changing faster than anyone can keep up with. A medication, a food additive, or a method of raising livestock that was safe yesterday is announced as unsafe today. We can no longer have an accurate world globe, because nations are changing their names and borders faster than we can manufacture the globes. I no more than learn how to work my computer, and I'm informed that it's out of date!

But wisdom is always useful. When we teach students *how* to think instead of *what* to think, then we are teaching them to be wise. No matter how knowledge changes, they will be able to handle life.

Biblical references to the wise refer not to persons with the right memorized answers, but to those who have a right relationship with God, with others, and with the earth.

These persons have an ability to make wise decisions and to locate the knowledge necessary for living.

Reflect

What flexibility is necessary for you to be wise in your teaching?

How can you help students to develop a right relationship with God? with others? with the earth?

Pray

God, sometimes I get hung up on imparting knowledge and forget about helping students develop wisdom. Make me wise, so that I can help others. Amen.

21
God, did you give me any talents?

There are different kinds of spiritual gifts, but they all come from the same Spirit. There are different ways to serve the same Lord, and we can each do different things. Yet the same God works in all of us and helps us in everything we do.
1 Corinthians 12:4-6 (Contemporary English Version)

"If only I could make nice bulletin boards."

"If only I could write on the board decently."

"If only I could tell a story the way the other teacher does."

"If only . . . If only . . . If only . . . "

None of us has the same set of talents. Some talents are very apparent, and some are rather obscure, requiring work to bring them out and develop them. Our talents are as varied as our fingertips. This is how God made us unique.

An anonymous person once wrote about someone: "She was pure joy, and she could only create unhappiness by being absent!" Now, that in itself is a talent. Some people's primary talent is to create joy for others. A student is blessed indeed when he or she has a teacher with that talent.

So often we forget about the talents of life that do not produce some particular thing that we can see, hear, taste, smell, or feel. We think of talents in terms of Rembrandt's paintings or Handel's choral works. We forget to bring our idea of talents down to every person. Or perhaps I should say that we forget to bring our idea of talents *up* to every person. The definition of talent is broader than the masterpieces.

God gave each of us talents, and if we haven't identified them and made use of them, then we are in debt to humankind and we are in debt to God.

Reflect

What talents has God given you that you haven't recognized as talents?

How can you better develop those talents?

Pray

God, I know that I am created uniquely. You gave me talents that I use each day, and talents that I am unaware of. Help me search out ways to develop my hidden talents and find ways to use them in service for you. Amen.

22
But I don't know the right words, my Lord.

The LORD God give me the right words to encourage the weary.
Isaiah 50:4a (Contemporary English Version)

Throughout our biblical heritage we find people who did not feel that they could speak the right words. It probably began when Adam and Eve hid from God, not knowing how to confess their wrongdoing. Abraham's servant asked God for the proper words when he went seeking a wife for Isaac. And Jacob was unsure how he should approach his brother, Esau, whom he had cheated many years before.

Moses tried to get out of his charge by saying that he didn't speak well. At first God gave him Aaron as his spokesperson. But soon Moses learned to rely on God to give him the words to say. In fact, in Deuteronomy there are pages and pages of instructions from the Lord that Moses spoke.

The prophet Jeremiah said, "I'm not a good speaker, Lord, and I'm too young." But God spoke great words through Jeremiah.

Jesus did not choose his disciples because they were great orators. Peter, who later was a primary force in the church, certainly felt himself inadequate before he received the Holy Spirit at Pentecost. He didn't even speak up and admit that he knew Jesus when Jesus was on trial.

Choosing the right words involves active listening. We cannot know how to talk to someone unless we know that person and really hear his or her needs. This involves vocally interpreting what you hear the person saying, and from time to time asking questions that help the person think more clearly.

The next step is to rely on God to speak words of support through you. Sometimes it helps to phrase briefly or to use a sentence prayer when you are searching for the proper words. I usually think my prayer in a personal way—something like, "OK, God. Here we go!" No matter how great our experience, it is God who must speak through us.

Reflect

What are some questions you might ask a person that would enable you to listen actively? (Examples: Do I hear you saying . . . ? Tell me a little more about what you're thinking.)

What is a brief prayer you might use to remind yourself to allow God to talk through you?

Pray

My God and helper, there are so many times when I feel inadequate to say the right words. I feel like Moses, unsure of my ability to speak. Or I sometimes feel young, like Jeremiah, certain that the persons to whom I'm speaking are far more mature in their faith than I. Help me to remember that although it is up to me to prepare ahead, you are the one ultimately responsible for speaking the words through me.

Let my words and my thoughts be pleasing to you, LORD, because you are my mighty rock and my protector. Amen.

Psalm 19:14 (Contemporary English Version)

23
There's much about you that I don't understand, God.

No one can explain how a baby breathes before it is born. So how can anyone explain what God does?

Ecclesiastes 11:5 (Contemporary English Version)

One of my students kept pressing me for a scientific explanation of God. I was teaching a high school class in the "God is dead" era. Finally I answered, "We don't know all there is to know about God, and we will never know it. After all, if we knew everything about God, then God wouldn't be God."

In definitions, I usually separate my faith from my beliefs. My faith is my relationship with God. My beliefs are the things that I believe, and they may change as I mature in my relationship with God. I no longer believe that God uses an ice pick to make holes in the clouds when it rains, as I did as a child.

My relationship with God must be built on trust, just as my relationships with people demand trust. When we take our seat on an airplane, do we know everything about the airline pilot or about the engineers and mechanics who worked on the plane? Do we know what goes on in the kitchens of the restaurants we frequent? Yet we trust those flying and repairing the plane and those preparing the food. If God made us and loves us, then how much more can we put our trust in our Maker than in some chef that a restaurant hires or some employee an airline approves.

And so I'm perfectly content to recognize that I don't know everything about God. That's why I am in such awe of God and why God's love for me is the greatest marvel of all.

Reflect

Think through your normal day. In what situations do you really trust other people with your own welfare or the welfare of your family?

As long as you believe that God loves you and wants the best for you, what "unknowns" about God can you simply trust?

Pray

God, help me allow you to be God and not feel that I must explain everything there is about you. Help me recognize that only you know all the answers. Amen.

My Cup Bubbles with Everyday Events

24
I praise you, God, for the many teachable moments.

Jesus looked up and saw some rich people tossing their gifts into the offering box. He also saw a poor widow putting in two pennies. And he said, "I tell you that this poor woman has put in more than all the others. Everyone else gave what they didn't need. But she is very poor and gave everything she had."

Luke 21:1-4 (Contemporary English Version)

Jesus was a master at recognizing and using teachable moments. He used fig trees (Luke 21:29), vineyards (Luke 20:9), salt and light (Matthew 5:13-14), seeds (Mark 4:26, 30), sheep (Matthew 18:12), and even a common meal (Matthew 26:26). Teachable moments are a treasurehouse of opportunities to share God spontaneously.

Discovering such moments takes an awareness that can be developed. The easiest teachable moments come through nature. Touch various textures, and thank God for feeling. Recognize that God could have made everything in black and white. Look for hidden treasures among the grasses, and listen to the sounds of insects in the darkness of night.

Teachable moments come about through events. As children outgrow their clothes, we recognize growth as a part of God's plan. Family dinners remind us of our heritage from the past. Any accomplishment can bring appreciation for the talents and abilities that God gave us. We grow in God's love when someone cares for us during a crisis. When someone cuts in front of us in traffic, we have the opportunity to ask God's blessing on them.

As you develop your recognition of teachable moments, you will discover an enrichment in your own faith. Soon you will see God everywhere—in nature, in friends, in students, and even as you drive through traffic.

Reflect

What teachable moments did you miss yesterday?

Think about your schedule for today or tomorrow. Where can you look for teachable moments?

Pray

God of the ordinary, keep me alert to the many opportunities to see you every day. Help me to live constantly in an awareness of you. Amen.

25
On the first day of classes, give me wisdom, Lord.

Jesus became wise, and he grew strong. God was pleased with him and so were the people.
Luke 2:52 (Contemporary English Version)

The first grader burst into the classroom and immediately had to show me his new pants. "The pants are my brother's," he said. "He grew too big for them, and I grew bigger to fit them!" I joined him in his pride, pointing out that he had grown, just as Jesus grew in the story that Luke wrote about Jesus' birth and childhood. This, I said, is all part of God's plan.

With the first day of classes, excitement runs high and we look forward to a new start. Children seem to have grown in height over the summer, and teens sport new dress styles along with their growth. Even adults recognize these new beginnings. We come to the first day of classes not only with excitement but also with a bit of awe: awe over the calling to teach and the responsibility that it brings.

As classes begin, we may be a little apprehensive about some students and how we can reach them. But we are dedicated to communicating our message. As we marvel over how each student has changed physically, we also ask God to help us teach the students so that they will grow in wisdom and in their understanding of God.

Reflect

Recall first days of classes when you were a child. What sort of sensations do you recall?

Think about just how this old statement will affect not only your students' lives but your life as well: *This is the first day of the rest of your life!*

Pray

Jesus, you know just what it's like to try to teach and sometimes feel you just aren't getting through to your students. Guide me as I begin this new time of learning with the students. Help me be a learner too. Amen.

26
Such joy in a child's face, Lord.

When I see the rainbow in the sky, I will always remember the promise that I have made to every living creature. The rainbow will be the sign of that solemn promise.

Genesis 9:16-17 (Contemporary English Version)

The young child was engrossed in the paints. He carefully moved the brush over the upper corner of his paper, leaving behind trails of yellow. "That's the sun," he declared with joy. "See how it shines down from the sky?"

Then he looked at the other paints. "I guess I'd better paint the sky blue," he said. The yellow brush went back into the jar, and the blue brush began its sweep across the other side of the page. On the fourth sweep of the brush, it crept over into the yellow of the sun. He stopped, with a startled expression on his face. The blue and the yellow had turned to green.

In that moment, I saw an awe of the unknown. A recognition of something great and beyond his understanding. And, I believe, in that moment there was worship—an awe of an incomprehensible power greater than himself. It reminded me that God could have made the world in black and white, and we would never have known the joy of colors. Yet God made color.

Reflect

When have you seen a child in awe of something he or she could not understand but recognized as wonderful?

Where can you recognize God's greatness in everyday life? How often do you overlook God, simply because you don't stop to see the colors?

Pray

My God, help me look for you in the colors, in the various textures you have made, and also in a child's expression of awe. May I become as that child, recognizing greatness even when I don't understand it. Amen.

27
You've given us so many ways to learn, Lord!

You created me and put me together. Make me wise enough to learn what you have commanded.
Psalm 119:73 (Contemporary English Version)

After a study on faith, the teens were asked to describe their own faith journey in some fashion. They were given the remaining class time to work on this. They would share their descriptions in the next class period.

During the next class, there were poems, stories, pictures, and even songs shared. One girl shared a brief interpretive dance she had created. Finally a quiet boy took his turn. He slowly reached into his pocket and pulled out a small box. Inside the box was a kernel of popcorn. He said, "My faith is like popcorn. It was hidden inside me until a real tough time made it explode, and now it's full and bright."

Such an array of ways to learn and understand faith we had! If we all learned through the spoken word, where would there be a need to create beautiful art? Or if we all learned through art, who would soothe us with music?

Reflect

What are the ways that Jesus used the seven intelligences to teach?

—Verbal-Linguistic, stories (Matthew 5:1-12)
—Logical-Mathematical, questions (Luke 22)
—Visual-Spatial, objects and pictures (Luke 6:47-49)
—Body-Kinesthetic, physical (John 13:1-17)
—Musical-Rhythmic (Matthew 26:30)
—Interpersonal, relationships (Mark 6:7-13)
—Intrapersonal, self-reflection (Mark 14:32-36)

What area do I need to grow in so that I'm well rounded?

Pray

God, thank you for the many ways to learn. Make me aware of these unique opportunities to teach so that others might learn. Amen.

28
Lord, is this really what teaching is about?

So during the meal Jesus got up, removed his outer garment, and wrapped a towel around his waist. He put some water into a large bowl. Then he began washing his disciples' feet and drying them with the towel he was wearing.

John 13:4-5 (Contemporary English Version)

I once heard a story of a duke who returned home after having been away for some time. As he got off the train a young woman stood among her luggage. Seeing the young man she said, "I'll pay my last shilling for someone to help carry my luggage to where I'm to work." The duke carried her luggage, right to his very own castle, where she was to begin her employment. When asked why he, who owned the castle, had done such a task, he said, "There is no service that is too menial."

At times when my day consists of cleaning up messy spills in the classroom or helping a child who has thrown up in the restroom, I ask, "Is this really what teaching is about?" Then I recall the story of the duke. I also remember the time that Jesus wrapped the towel around his waist and washed his friends' feet, one of the most menial tasks of his day, one usually done by a servant.

Reflect

Do I "expect" certain privileges because I am a teacher? Why?

What act of service do I find most difficult to carry out?

Pray

Master Servant, help me realize that when Jesus became a servant he exemplified the ultimate in service. Help me remember that there is no service that love cannot carry out. Amen.

29
Lord, purify me and make me clean.

Wash me with hyssop* until I am clean and whiter than snow.
Create pure thoughts in me and make me faithful again.
Psalm 51:7, 10 (Contemporary English Version)

As I washed another set of tempera paint-covered hands, I wondered just how many hands I'd washed in my life. Some days it seems endless for preschool teachers, either washing hands or supervising the child's attempt at handwashing. And a seemingly endless line of scraped knees, elbows, and chins must be cleansed and treated.

The Bible mentions some form of the word *wash* 124 times, besides the many references to cleanliness. It is interesting, however, that progressively through our biblical heritage we have grown from the belief that *we* must make ourselves clean before the Lord, to an understanding of God (and Christ, in the New Testament) as the cleansing agent.

Although I tire of the washing process, I will remember that God never tires of cleansing us. God stands by with a wet, cool cloth, ready for us to turn over our hurts and our

*The psalmist refers to the herb hyssop because in that day the branches of this small bush were used as a symbol of cleansing from sin.

bruises, our mistakes and our blunders. God chooses not to take away the pain, but God does forgive us and prepare us for the healing process. Of course, we must allow God to do this. We must willingly open up our clenched fists, and hold up our skinned knees and elbows and chins, admitting that we blundered or fell.

Reflect

What mistakes and bruises do you have that need washing clean?

How can you help others recognize God's earnest desire to cleanse us?

Pray

Lord, each time I wash my own hands or wash another's mistakes or bruises, help me to remember that you stand by with soap and towel in hand, just waiting to wash me clean. Amen.

30
I see care and love in their eyes, Lord.

The baby's older sister stood off at a distance to see what would happen to him (Moses).
Exodus 2:4 (Contemporary English Version)

There was a true expression of love in the child's eyes as she led her little brother into the room. "This is Peter," she said. "He's special. He's my brother."

This was Peter's first year to be a part of our midweek program, and Wanda watched over him with pride. She gave him a kiss as she left and said she would come for him at break time.

True to her word, she was standing beside the door when we took the children out to play. She held Peter's hand as we walked to the playground, and then watched him from her play group throughout the period. After the break Wanda walked her brother back to the room and skipped off to her class.

Observing the love and care that Wanda gave Peter reminded me of Miriam's care for Moses when he was hidden in the river. What pride Miriam must have had, years later, when Moses gathered the people and led them out of bondage. We don't know much about Miriam in the intervening years, but we do know that she assisted and supported him during the exodus.

My cup runneth over when I see God's love so naturally displayed through a child.

Reflect

Where have I seen God's love through my students?

How can I express God's love to my students?

Pray

God of Moses and Miriam, thank you for giving us the ability to express love and care. I recognize that you made us with a need for such love from other persons. Help me to find ways to express that love. Amen.

31
O God, please find me when I'm lost.

I have learned to feel safe and satisfied, just like a young child on its mother's lap.

Psalm 131:2 (Contemporary English Version)

The toddler stood in the middle of the room, rivers of tears running down her face. She had mashed her finger with a toy, and any amount of consolation from the teacher did not help. When her mother arrived, however she climbed into her lap and soon settled into a blissful sleep.

The mother's comforting lap reminded me of the psalmist's suggestion that we be content with God as a child is with his or her mother in the midst of trauma. The mother did not make the hurt finger better. The finger continued to throb and remain red, even after an application of ice. But the security and comfort of the mother's lap made the pain endurable.

The same is true with God. God does not automatically make our world one of sunshine and roses with no problems. But when troubles come, we are secure and comforted if we draw near to God and recognize the mother's love that is readily available for us.

Reflect

When have I ignored God's motherly love? When have I allowed God's love to wash over me?

What trauma is happening in my students' lives? How can I share God's motherly love with them?

Pray

O God of great motherly love, help me recognize your love and share it with others. Amen.

32
You show yourself in many ways, Lord.

May the grace of the Lord Jesus Christ, and the love of God, and the fellowship of the Holy Spirit be with you all.
2 Corinthians 13:14 (New International Version)

When I was a child, my pride and joy was a large box of forty-eight crayons with so many colors I couldn't even remember all the names. And then someone told me that all those colors came from three primary colors: red, blue, and yellow. How could this be? So many from three?

In the same way, I had difficulty recognizing just how God could be three-in-one or the Trinity. Now I realize that children think very concretely, and as a child I was not yet prepared to grasp the abstract.

The Trinity is never actually named in the Bible. However, because of the three ways that God comes to us, the people in the early centuries of the Christian church developed the doctrine of the Trinity as a human interpretation of divine activity. And so, we can recognize the deity as coming to us as our creator/sustainer, in human form, and acting within us. At specific times we may encounter our deity more fully in one form or another. But we recognize that God is one god and forever to be praised!

Reflect

When do you most often feel that God comes to you as creator/sustainer? as "God with skin on"? as a spirit within you?

Is there any part of life that you cannot see covered by these three divine activities?

Pray

God, my creator, my savior, and my guide, I ask that you show me the many ways to relate to you. Help my faltering understanding of your vast connectional power. Amen.

33
No, not again! Do you will such violence, Lord?

My friends, you were chosen to be free. So don't use your freedom as an excuse to do anything you want. Use it as an opportunity to serve each other with love.

Galatians 5:13 (Contemporary English Version)

With disbelief I watched television scenes of the aftermath of a violent shooting in a public school. I wondered what sorts of issues those students were wrestling with. I wonder what sorts of issues all students must wrestle with today. As I spoke to several students I understood the lack of security that they felt at school. Then the primary question came out, *Why does God do this to innocent people?*

I cannot believe that the God of love that I know would bring about such violence intentionally. I can't believe that God would decide, *I will make that child take a gun to school and shoot several students so that other students will learn a lesson.*

Leslie Weatherhead, in his little book *The Will of God,* suggested that we view God's will as three different wills: intentional, circumstantial, and ultimate. The *intentional* will includes God's goodness, as the best parent we know would want to bring about for the child. And a part of that intentional will is that we be created in God's image with individual wills of our own. But unwanted events happen, especially when we follow our own wills without consulting God. Those circumstances bring about the *circumstantial* will of God. Under those conditions, which we willingly or unwillingly create, God usually does not step in. We, or someone else, must suffer the consequences, such as the violent shootings. Weatherhead's final will of God is the *ultimate* will. Although the unintentional has happened, if we allow God to work through the circumstances, we will come out stronger in our relationship with God than we were before.

My God is a caring God. With each day I grow to appreciate this more and more. I feel that God weeps with us when such violence happens, and God waits with open arms to comfort us.

Reflect

What sorts of unwelcome circumstances have your students encountered? How can you love them through it?

How can you share Leslie Weatherhead's ideas about God's will with a student?

Pray

Direct me, O Lord, in ways that I can help my students to recognize your love no matter what the circumstances. Remind me of that love again and again. Amen.

34
Thank you for our senses, Lord.

O taste and see that the LORD is good; happy are those who take refuge in [God].

Psalm 34:8 (New Revised Standard Version)

As I taught a class of young children, I watched them direct everything they got their hands on into their mouths. The toddlers were exploring the world with all five senses, including taste!

Each sense is important for us to experience all of life. Sight is the most common, but those who have lost the use of sight tell us that with the loss of one sense the other senses become even more sensitive. Sounds help us recall places and events, and I certainly recognize the importance and the sense of smell when I burn some food I'm cooking on the stove!

Touch brings mind to body. In many instances the sense of taste binds all our senses together. When we smell something delightful we can almost taste it before the food reaches our lips. The sight, sound, smell, and feel of the ocean spray remain incomplete without the taste of salt air.

Scientists, however, overlook the sixth, most important sense in our lives. For lack of a better word, I call it the sense of soul filling. This inner sense completes our unity with God and all that God has given us. Sometimes we find this sixth sense through complete quiet and solitude. At other times we experience soul filling through other people, through community.

We also find this sixth sense through teaching. It is not something that can be experienced through any other sense. God places it within us, and our soul grows with each encounter we have with our students.

Reflect

When, in the past week, have you felt this sixth sense?

When have you felt your soul filled by God?

Pray

Lord, fill my soul with your love. Direct me in your paths throughout my day so that I might fully experience you. Amen.

35
Lord, thank you for the gift of sleep.

You surely know that your own body is a temple where the Holy Spirit lives. The Spirit is in you and is a gift from God. You are no longer your own. God paid a great price for you. So use your body to honor God.
1 Corinthians 6:19-20 (Contemporary English Version)

The lesson plan just did not seem to fall into place, and the eyelids continued to fall shut. I found myself praying, "God, you know I have to get this finished for tomorrow. Why won't you keep these eyes open?"

Finally, I closed the book, turned out the light, and gave in to sleep. I set the alarm for an hour early and began a breath prayer. I formed the sentence in my mind and repeated it each time I slowly breathed in and out. "Give me clearness of mind, O God."

I awoke the next morning, refreshed and thinking clearly. I sat down to the lesson plan, and within twenty minutes it was finished. As I paused to thank God for sleep and a clear mind, I recalled the suggestion someone had given me several years before, that sleep is God's gift to us. God could have made our bodies so that they would not need sleep. But God chose to create us so that we need that "down time" to rejuvenate our bodies. And so sleep is a gift from God: a time of refreshment, a time of relaxation, a time of release.

Much in teaching depends on a clear mind. There are plans to be made, circumstances when plans must be adjusted, teachable moments to grasp, and emergencies to be confronted. Our brains are actual physical organs and require care, just as our teeth require care. Without the proper sleep they can't function as well.

Reflect

Will it make a difference in your life if you wait until morning to hear the television news? What can you adjust in your evening schedule so that you can get more sleep?

Create a breath prayer to use as you fall asleep.

Pray

God, thank you for the gift of sleep. It brings me closer to you. Amen.

My Cup Is Filled by Others

36
My God, how wide is your love?

I want you to know all about Christ's love, although it is too wonderful to be measured. Then your lives will be filled with all that God is.

Ephesians 3:19 (Contemporary English Version)

How do you measure a cup full of love? How do you measure a heart full of love?

When our children were quite young, they became restless while traveling in the car. We began to answer their "How much longer till we get there?" questions by holding our thumb and finger up in a measurement and saying, "About that long." Because their understanding had not matured enough to really understand measurement and time, this simple answer satisfied them. In fact, it satisfied them even more than if we had told them the exact amount of time. However, by the next year's vacation trip, they had learned enough about time that such an answer was no longer accepted.

Paul, when writing to the Ephesians, found it baffling to try to measure love, especially Christ's love. How can we explain such love to students who are inexperienced in the concept of measurements? All children learn best by experience, and that is the only way I know to explain God's love. We must help our students *experience* that love, through us and through one another, even if they are too young to understand it. And adults will understand and accept God's love better if they also experience it first.

Paul was right as he continued in his letter, "Then your lives will be filled with all that God is."

Reflect

When have you experienced God's love so full that your cup ran over?

What can you do to help your students experience the fullness of God's love?

Pray

God, your love is wide and long and high and deep, fully immeasurable. Help me experience that love and pass it on to others. Amen.

37
Lord, why can't we accept our differences?

Honor God by accepting each other, as Christ has accepted you.
Romans 15:7 (Contemporary English Version)

In my early morning stupor I heard the news, but I could not believe what I was hearing. A young girl had actually killed herself because over the years she had been ridiculed and laughed at for her weight. And just two days prior to that I'd heard that there is evidence that obesity is now considered a disease, not just a matter of diet.

I recalled students in classes I had taught. It seems that there is always a student who gets the brunt of the jokes. Sometimes they seem to shrug it off like rainwater on a duck, and sometimes it obviously affects their ego. However, we never know how much they hurt inside. When I was growing up we called it sarcasm and thought we were really smart to be able to bat sarcastic remarks around. Now the remarks are labeled "put-downs," which is a little more realistic of what they do to people. But no matter what we label them, such remarks can cut to the core causing the victim to "bleed" internally, even draining all desire to live.

But there is more to acceptance of persons than avoiding such cutting remarks. If we take Paul's words to the

Romans seriously, we will recognize that accepting others, no matter who, and speaking only kind words are actually a way of praising God. After all, God created that person. By putting down a person, we are actually saying that God created something bad. But God does not make junk!

Jesus saw good in each person he met. He even saw beneath the tough exterior of Peter and knew he would become a firm foundation for the church. He also recognized the worth of women, of persons of other faiths, and of persons with undesirable lifestyles. Can we afford to do any less?

Reflect

When have you observed someone ridiculing someone else? Have you adopted the "kids will be kids" attitude or stepped out to do something about it?

Remember that, in such situations, by not speaking up for the person you actually condone the unchristian actions. If you had the chance to relive such opportunities to affirm the person, what would you do?

Pray

God, help me remember that my actions tell who I am. Amen.

38
Lord, thank you for children who point the way.

Then he said, "I promise you this. If you don't change and become like a child, you will never get into the kingdom of heaven."

Matthew 18:3 (Contemporary English Version)

The young girl's head was bent low as she concentrated on a drawing. Everyone else was working on their math assignment, and as the teacher walked down the aisle the girl hastily slipped the paper under her desk. When the teacher saw her unfinished math paper, she spoke to her sternly about wasting her time and then moved on to the back of the room. The young girl pulled the drawing out and hastily added several words to the page.

That whole morning had been particularly stressful, and the teacher was at wit's end. In fact, the children seemed to sense that something was wrong. The bell rang for lunch, and the students placed their math assignments on the teacher's desk as they left the room. As the teacher picked up the math papers something fell to the floor. It was a drawing of a flower and a bright sun in the corner. Across the bottom were only five words, "I'm praying for you today." No signature, just those five simple words.

Reflect

Do you let others know that God has brought their problems to your mind? Send a postcard to someone for whom you are praying.

When have you learned a truth or been reminded of a ministry by a child?

Pray

Our Lord, through Jesus you taught us to become as children. It's so easy to slip into grown-up ways! Thank you for the reminders. Amen.

39
God, give me understanding for my students.

Our Lord, by your wisdom you made so many things; the whole earth is covered with your living creatures.
Psalm 104:24 (Contemporary English Version)

Sometimes it baffles me when I look around the classroom and see the variety in my students. They vary in their appearance, in their alertness to learning, and even in their methods of learning. I can teach the same thing in three different ways, and there are always some students who grasp it in one form but not another. When there is a crisis in the classroom, I can depend on certain students responding immediately and others waiting for someone else to attend to the situation.

We've always known that physical appearances depend on the genes we receive. And today's psychologists are finding that more of our characteristics are inherited than was previously believed.

I recall a statement by a woman in our church when I was in high school. She said, "Variety is the spice of life, and I like mine very spicy!" Sometimes I wish that there was less variety so that I would know just what to expect, or so that I only had to teach with the methods that I enjoy using. But maybe this is why we are so fearful of cloning. If we were all alike, who would do the bookkeeping (which I hate) and who would cook meals for our church dinners (which my husband enjoys cooking)?

In all of God's wisdom, we are made in various forms.

Reflect

Think for a moment about yourself and a sibling or other close relative. How are you different, in physical appearance, personality, and your likes and dislikes?

Think of students in your class and list the positive characteristics in various students, differences that are good.

Pray

I thank you, God, for the variety you have put in this world. Especially I thank you for the variety in people. Each person is so different, yet each was made by you in a specific design. How varied is your creation! Amen.

40
Such a gift she has from you, Lord.

Each of you has been blessed with one of God's many wonderful gifts to be used in the service of others. So use your gift well.
1 Peter 4:10 (Contemporary English Version)

Susan's grades started out well that year, but then they began to slip. Soon she was far behind in her work. It just seemed she didn't get around to it. "Why don't you get your work done?" I asked.

"I don't have time," she answered. "I help Marsha when she needs to go to the bathroom or she gets lost. I also help her with her lessons. No one else cares about Marsha." Marsha was a mentally challenged child in her class.

I began to observe Susan more closely. She seemed to have a sixth sense for finding persons who needed help. Any time someone fell on the playground, Susan was always there to help brush the child off. When a child struggled with a reading assignment, Susan offered encouragement.

I began to realize that this was truly a gift from God, to be able to sense the needs of others and to step forth to help meet those needs. She found fulfillment in using her gift. This was evident in the joy that shone in her face. Some years later, Susan told me that her greatest desire was not to have an executive career, not to earn a doctorate, but to recognize others' needs and to meet those needs.

Reflect

Whom do you know who has this gift of recognizing needs and fulfilling them?

Is this a gift that can be cultivated? How can you nurture the gift in yourself and in others?

Pray

Lord, my cup runneth over with joy when I see persons like Susan. There are many who allow such a gift to lie dormant. How can I encourage them to use this great gift which you have given them? Amen.

41
Is my teaching really making a difference, God?

You are like light for the whole world. A city built on top of a hill cannot be hidden, and no one would light a lamp and put it under a clay pot. A lamp is placed on a lampstand, where it can give light to everyone in the house. Make your light shine, so that others will see the good that you do and will praise your Father in heaven.

Matthew 5:14-16 (Contemporary English Version)

There are days in teaching when I really wonder if I am making a difference. The student leaves the classroom in a whirlwind, or chattering with a friend, seemingly indifferent about what I have spent hours trying to prepare.

But once a man told me that an idea I had casually thrown out in a discussion months before had made all the difference in his thinking about that subject. I hardly recalled the discussion. In fact, I had thought that he was so determined in his view that he would never question it.

In the seventh chapter of Acts we read of the stoning of Stephen. Paul (who was then Saul) held the coats of those who stoned this follower of Christ, and heard his statement to the council members.

Prior to that, Paul had been a student of Gamaliel (Acts 22:3), whose remarks, recorded in the fifth chapter of Acts, advised the political powers that "if what they [the followers of Christ] are planning is something of their own doing, it will fail. But if God is behind it, you cannot stop it anyway, unless you want to fight against God" (5:38-39 Contemporary English Version). We have no idea how God used Paul's teacher and the experience of Stephen's stoning to make him receptive to Christ's message, but it surely must have made an impact.

You may never realize how your teaching fits into the puzzle of a student's life. But you can be sure that God uses all things for good when we follow our calling.

Reflect

What actions and attitudes of yours will make a positive impression on a student's life?

How can you be aware of negative actions and change them to positive?

Pray

God, help me recognize that every day I am a part of the puzzle of someone else's life. I may not understand how, but I know that you can take the pieces and make a lovely mosaic for your glory. Help me become a bright puzzle piece in the lives of my students. Amen.

42
And the world goes round and round!

People come, and people go, but still the world never changes.
Ecclesiastes 1:4 (Contemporary English Version)

My concept of time changed when I realized that children I had taught were now becoming teachers themselves. Could this be possible? Did this mean that I was getting older? I read the first chapter of Ecclesiastes and felt about as useless as the author, who saw life as fruitless. Then I received a letter that helped me see the fourth verse of that chapter in a little different light.

Sometime back I had asked a young couple to consider leading a college age group in our church. I met with them and told them just why I felt they were ideal persons for the job. I asked them to pray about the possibility and told them that I would call them in a few days. When I called they said they felt that God was urging them at least to try the venture. Soon after they began their ministry, I moved out of town. I was concerned because I wouldn't be there to give them the encouragement they should have.

Now, four years later, here was a letter to me thanking me for asking them to work with the college students. They stated that this had been the most rewarding experience they had had in their Christian walk. Sure enough, I'd come to that church and I'd left, but it continued to be a caring and supporting church, affirming their leaders through their ministry. People come and people go, but the love of the world still carries on. That love isn't dependent on me, for it is placed there by God.

Reflect

Where do you see God's love breaking through, even in unpredictable times?

What does this say about God's dependable self? What other situations point to the dependability of God and God's world?

Pray

My God, I see your dependability about me everywhere I turn. It shines through love, through seasons, through the miracle of birth, and even through death. Help me learn to rely on your plan and trust that it will come about. Amen.

43
Lord, there's much to love about each student.

People judge others by what they look like, but I judge people by what is in their hearts.

1 Samuel 16:7*b *(Contemporary English Version)

It's a practice I've tried to carry out when I've taught: dividing the students into five groups and assigning each group to one weekday. Each day I concentrate my prayers on the individuals assigned for that day. As I set up my list, I add something specific that will call that person to mind, something as simple as "Juanita, whose hair always seems to be in her eyes." During the year I might change the representation to something I've learned about the person or some recognized need of the student.

One year I had a particularly difficult class. It seemed that at least half of the students enjoyed making snide comments and put-downs. I tried to find affirmative statements to add to my prayer list for those students, but continually I felt blocked. Finally, the director of the program and I prayed about it. Through shared prayer, my heart began to overflow with love for the unruly students. I recognized that their lives would be unhappy if they continued in this manner. I also came to acknowledge that although God was unhappy with the students' actions, God continued to love them. This was something positive that I could write on the list, that each was loved by God.

Subsequently, the whole staff launched a "put down put-downs" emphasis and discovered that some of the students actually did not recognize how hurting put-downs can be to other people. Our efforts paid off, and the effect was even felt in the public school.

Reflect

What student do you know who needs your recognition of God's love?

Try praying for your students in this manner for six weeks, and then review your attitude toward each student.

Pray

My cup does overflow with love, O God, when I recognize how much you love. It overflows with love for you, and then the love spreads to others. Thank you for your love, and help me share it. Amen.

44
Help me keep my students' confidence, my God.

A gossip tells everything, but a true friend will keep a secret.
Proverbs 11:13 (Contemporary English Version)

As teachers, we sometimes learn things about people that we really wish we didn't know. A student may tell us something in confidence, or we may have someone else tell us about a student.

Jesus exhibited how we should act when the Pharisees brought the adulteress before him. He told them that the person who had not sinned should be the one to cast the first stone. Jesus also spoke to the woman. When the others left, he told her that he didn't accuse her and asked her to live her life differently (John 8:3-10).

I have a small white stone with sharp edges that I keep on my bookshelf beside my desk. On it is written the word "First." It reminds me of this encounter that the desperate woman had with Jesus.

There are times when we should report an injustice, but we are not trained psychologists. How can we know the difference in being a gossip or a "tattletale" and responsible reporting?

Reflect

Think about something you have heard about someone: Test what you have heard against these thoughts:

- Does it involve an injustice rather than idle gossip?
- Does it cause physical damage to a person?
- Does it cause emotional damage to a person?
- Does it cause damage to property?

If your answer to any of these is yes, you may want to investigate the situation.

Pray

God, you are a caring God. There are times when I may need to help carry out justice through reporting something. Enable me to determine those times, and to keep my mouth shut at other times. Amen.

45
God, help me affirm others.

You can see the speck in your friend's eye. But you don't notice the log in your own eye. How can you say, "My friend, let me take the speck out of your eye," when you don't see the log in your own eye? You showoffs! First, get the log out of your own eye. Then you can see how to take the speck out of your friend's eye.

Luke 6:41-42 (Contemporary English Version)

Often when we see someone excel in something, our own inferior self begins to work double time trying to find something done poorly. Instead of complimenting the person on the things done well, we probe into the corners and come up with something not quite up to par. Then we bravely wave it out for everyone to see, as if we'd just beheaded a dragon!

In essence, we're saying, "See, that person isn't so great! I may be inferior, but I can find something that makes that person look bad too!"

I read of a fifteen-year veteran teacher. The supervisor observed her teaching and told her that her teaching was very good. The teacher was moved to tears, because in her fifteen years of teaching she had never had a professional educator to tell her that she was doing a good job.

Granted, there were probably minor areas in which the

teacher could have improved. The supervisor could have pulled up one of those and waved it in her face. But by complimenting the teacher on her ability, the supervisor exhibited competence in supervising. My guess is that the teacher tried even harder to do a good job, and that she felt confident to approach the supervisor for help or advice. The teacher had not been cut down to size, but rather brought up to the supervisor's size. They both benefited from the experience.

Reflect

How might you affirm the actions of your students?

Do you know teachers who need affirming? Make a point to affirm them.

Pray

Dear God, help me realize, when I start to point out an insignificant mistake, that I've made many mistakes in my life too. Amen.

46
God, I can't believe that you never give us up.

What can we say about all this? If God is on our side, can anyone be against us?

Romans 8:31 (Contemporary English Version)

I watched as the students played ball. It was only a pickup game, but William, one of the youngest students, was having difficulty hitting the ball. Julio, the oldest student, was pitching the ball and continued to pitch it to Willie even after he swung the bat at thin air three times. One of the students in the outfield began to complain, "He's had his turn at bat. Three strikes and you're out!"

But Julio simply turned to the complainer and said, "This is a for-fun game, and Willie's not having fun if he doesn't get to hit the ball. We're not giving up on him. That's how you learn."

Julio continued to pitch the ball, moving a little closer each time. Finally the ball and bat made contact, and Willie's smile spread from ear to ear. That young boy will never forget how the older boy refused to give up on him. Julio was unaware of it, but he was laying a firm foundation for Willie's understanding of the steadfast love of God.

Sometimes we make God very sad with our actions, but

God never gives up on us, no matter how much we goof. And God wants us to "do right" not so that we receive love, but rather *because* we love.

How great a God! Can you imagine any love more wonderful than to be loved into loving? With such a God loving us, can anyone really be against us? That unending love sustains us, no matter what happens. And the love comes simply because God loves, not because of anything that we have done.

Reflect

When have you felt like giving up on a student who was struggling? How did you react?

Which of your students are particularly trying of your patience? Write the names of those students down and try praying for them daily for a month.

Pray

God, you never give up when even one of us has strayed. Help me exhibit that steadfast love to my students. Amen.

47
Lord, I feel as if I'm betrayed.

My enemies are not the ones who sneer and make fun. I could put up with that or even hide from them. But it was my closest friend, the one I trusted most.

Psalm 55:12-13 (Contemporary English Version)

Fair weather friends" some people call them. These are the people who are friends when it is convenient, but when the going gets rough they jump ship.

And then there are the friendships of politics. These persons are friends as long as the relationship profits them, but if there is no profit they find some other "friendship" that is more profitable.

Unfortunately, as teachers, we often encounter such "friends." Jesus, the greatest teacher of all, dealt with such relationships between his disciples as well as experiencing himself the brunt of betrayal and denial.

As the psalmist concludes his psalm, he says, "Our LORD, we belong to you. We tell you what worries us, and you won't let us fall" (v. 22). We know that God understands our problems. God may not take them away, but God "won't let us fall" beyond the point of no return. The psalmist always returns to hope, no matter how despondent he may seem, because hope is in God.

Reflect

When have you felt betrayed? Did you share your problems with God? Learn the prayer below and pray it (or one similar) next time you feel betrayed.

When have you unintentionally ignored someone and discovered later that the person felt you betrayed him or her? How can you keep this from happening in the future?

Pray

God, you understand how I feel when I'm betrayed. I need your love now. Lift me up and set me straight! Amen.

48
Lord, you are always with me.

Where could I go to escape from your Spirit or from your sight? If I were to climb up to the highest heavens, you would be there. If I were to dig down to the world of the dead you would also be there. Suppose I had wings like the dawning day and flew across the ocean. Even then your powerful arm would guide and protect me.

Psalm 139:7-10 (Contemporary English Version)

Anyone who has taught or raised preschoolers has probably experienced the joy of reading the story *Runaway Bunny,* by Margaret Wise Brown.

The story quite simply tells of a baby bunny who informs his mother that he will run away. Her response is always the same: she will be with him no matter where he goes. If the bunny becomes a rock on a mountain, she will become a mountain climber and climb up to him. If he becomes a sailboat in the great sea, she will become the wind that blows him. Even if the bunny becomes a bird and flies away, the mother will be a tree that the bunny will come home to.

This little story does not have a "religious" word in it, but it still lays a foundation for recognizing God's love-you-anyway grace that is with us no matter where we go or what we do.

Reflect

Read the psalm passage above and think about how God is like a loving parent, always anxious to be with us and to help us.

Think of other stories that have an underlying truth that is basic to your faith. How might you use *Runaway Bunny* and other stories in your teaching?

Pray

My God, you are like a loving parent to me: ever caring, always with me, and anxious to be the wind for my sails. Amen.

49
I need some joy in my life, Lord.

There are many who pray: "Give us more blessings, O Lord. Look on us with kindness!"

But the joy that you have given me is more than they will ever have with all their grain and wine.

Psalm 4:6-7 (Today's English Version)

I looked around the classroom, reflecting on the students. I knew some troubling things about several of them. One in particular had some real trauma going on in her life right now. I didn't see how she could be happy. Yet a radiance came from her face, and she answered a fellow classmate's question with a smile, really anxious to share her faith with him.

Then I realized that there is a difference between happiness and joy. This student's life was not happy, by any means. But her face and her voice exhibited joy, the depth of which only comes from God. Happiness comes from the outside, usually from our material surroundings. Happiness is only temporary, and often what brings us happiness in one moment becomes mundane the next.

But joy comes from the inside. True joy comes about when we open ourselves to God and allow God to work through us and to direct our lives. The peace of knowing that we are in God's direction brings us joy. And the best way to come to that joy is to spend one-on-one time with our God.

Reflect

Does the joy of living with God show through my life?

How can I build quiet reflective times into my lesson so that my students begin to develop joy?

Pray

O God of joy, amid the commercials for cars and toys, help me recognize what brings about true joy. Help me share that joy with my students and others whom I encounter each day. Amen.

50
O my God, why am I afraid of failure?

God is our mighty fortress, always ready to help in times of trouble.

Psalm 46:1 (Contemporary English Version)

Maria sat at the table, simply staring into space. Before her lay the materials for a project she was making. I approached and asked if she had decided just what she was going to do with the materials. She smiled up at me and began to bubble with her plans. I told her that I thought it was a nice project and I was sure she would do a good job. Suddenly her face lost its smile and she said, "But I'm afraid to start. What if I can't do it? Or what if I spend all that time and mess up the materials and it turns out terrible?"

Maria was afraid to dive into her project for fear of failure. She never will experience the thrill of accomplishment unless she begins. I thought about how often we adults miss out on great experiences because we are afraid that we will fail. Is this why the first two chapters of a novel have lain in my file drawer for ten years? Am I afraid I'll bomb out? Is this why I never learned to ride a bike? Afraid that I couldn't accomplish it?

No matter how hard the job seems, we can know that God will be there to give us strength. Should we fail, God will help us to simply turn the failure into a learning experience.

Reflect

What project am I afraid to begin for fear of failure?

How can I break the project down into mini-goals and set about achieving one goal at a time?

Pray

You are my partner in these projects, God. Be my mighty fortress, as the psalmist asked. I count on you as I forge ahead, pushing the fear of failure aside. Amen.

51
Lord, send someone to show me the way.

You also know we did everything for you that parents would do for their own children. We begged, encouraged, and urged each of you to live in a way that would honor God.
1 Thessalonians 2:11-12**a** ***(Contemporary English Version)***

Until recent years, we seldom heard a reference to mentoring. We are finding, however, that a faith mentor is beneficial to all of us. As a teacher, you are likely to be a model for some student, and there may even be opportunity for you to be a mentor.

There are several biblical incidents of mentoring, although that exact word is not used. Moses was a mentor for Aaron. Eli was Samuel's mentor. Mary spent some time with her cousin, Elizabeth, apparently deepening her understanding of her role in God's plan. Jesus himself was a prime example of a mentor, forever encouraging his followers to dig deeper and find a richer relationship with God.

Modeling and mentoring have been compared to a seminar and a consultation. The seminar is general in nature and lays out a direction. You choose to follow that direction or some variation of the proposed direction. A consultation is more personalized and takes on a one-to-one relationship. The direction is geared to the needs of the individual.

As we search out models and recognize ourselves as models, we are forced to look at our lives and reflect on our roles in God's world. Mentors help us explore possible roles. The mentor acts as a guide or resource person, not giving solutions and answers, but helping us search for our own direction.

Reflect

When have I been a model for someone else? When has my action not been worthy of modeling?

Whom might I ask to help me as a mentor?

Pray

God, it is my desire to grow in my faith. Sometimes I need someone with whom I can bounce ideas and thoughts. And I need someone to keep me on course when I become lazy in my prayer life. Guide me to the right person. Amen.

52
Lord, make me an instrument of your love.

Nevertheless I am continually with you; you hold my right hand. You guide me with your counsel, and afterward you will receive me with honor.

Psalm 73:23-24 (New Revised Standard Version)

I pulled up to the traffic light, and the bumper sticker caught my eye: "If you can read this, thank a teacher." My first reaction was, "Yes! I can identify with that! We teachers DO make a difference."

However, before I had a chance to burst my buttons with pride, I remembered that long ago I dedicated my teaching to God. I asked God to speak through my teaching. I wonder if I can really claim to make the difference in my students myself if God is truly speaking through me. When do I give God the glory?

We were taught to graciously receive a compliment. If we brush a compliment off then we are sending the message that the person offering the praise does not have good judgment. Yet, everything that we are or do is actually a gift from God. God not only made us, but also gave us the talents and mental gifts to accomplish our tasks. How can we accept compliments and still acknowledge God's part in our achievements? Perhaps we can say something like, "Thank you, and I thank God for helping me to accomplish it."

As I reflect on the bumper sticker now, I realize that I must back down from my prideful self. Instead, I can pray a prayer, "Thank you, God, for using me as an instrument for your loving care."

Now I'm looking for the bumper sticker that says,

If you can read and understand this,
then as a teacher I thank God for guidance.

Reflect

Have you asked God to use your teaching as an instrument?

Consider some phrases that will let others know that you consider yourself as an instrument of God.

Pray

God, thank you for influencing others through me. Forgive the times I exhibit such a casual manner about your part in my life. Amen.